BARRY WHITE
THE ICON IS LOVE

ISBN 0-7935-4382-7

7777 W. BLUEMOUND RD. P.O. BOX 13819 MILWAUKEE, WI 53213

"I believe that some people are children of destiny," says musical icon Barry White. "No matter how they try to mess it up, they have a destiny. Believe me, I tried to mess it up . . . I was a gangbanger by the time I was 10, went to jail when I was 16, and I even tried to quit doing music altogether one time. But my destiny has been music since I was 5 years old . . ."

It's been a long way from his wayward early years to becoming the man who in 1994 has delivered one of his most exciting projects in years, the new album "The Icon Is Love."

The young Barry White was feared and respected; with his younger brother Darryl he ruled his neighborhood turf and turned to crime when his teenage love broke his heart. The same young Barry was director of the local church choir and had read the Bible, the Koran and the Kabbalah by the time he was 11, and later became a tough gangbanger who never should have made it out of the 'hood, let alone become music's Love Man. This is the same Barry White who had—at last count—107 gold and platinum records from every corner of the globe, the same man who has traveled from Dubai to Chile, from Trinidad to Australia. The transformation from '50s street hoodlum to '70s hit maker to '90s icon has had its share of funny, sad, happy and bad times...

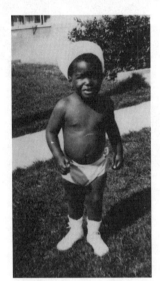

Barry was enthralled as a child by the music played in his own household by his mother, everything from Bach to blues. Influenced by the likes of Johnny Otis, Miles Davis, Bo Diddley, Jesse Belvin, Tito Puente, Nina Simone, the Coasters and John Coltrane, Barry launched his career in those early years by singing with streetwise groups like the Upfronts, the Atlantics and the Majestics.

By the '60s, Barry was trying to make ends meet for his wife and four kids, collecting welfare checks, constantly on the move. He enjoyed a stint traveling through the South as tour manager and drummer with '60s hit maker Jackie Lee ("The Duck"). Finally, he stayed put in L.A. long enough to ask industry veteran Bob Keene, who'd had a hand in the careers of Sam Cooke and Ritchie Valens, the key question: "What's an A&R man?" and landed that very gig with Keene's company.

Barry experienced his first taste of success when three of his productions, with singer Felice Taylor, made the British charts in 1967. He stepped out on his own a few years later when longtime partner, best friend, and spiritual adviser Larry Nunes encouraged him to create his own pathway in music. He soon discovered a trio of female singers and, naming them Love Unlimited, Barry

began a golden journey to worldwide chart success in 1972 when the group's first single, "Walkin' In The Rain With The One I Love" went gold. Soon Nunes begged Barry to put his own distinctive bass voice on some tracks he was preparing for another male vocalist. Barry finally gave in and, fusing the classics and the gospel music of his youth, created his own sensual sound. His arranging prowess helped create the unparalleled Love Unlimited Orchestra, with its French horns, violas, violins, harps, cellos—a unique blend that mixed soul music with strings.

Barry's romantic sound astounded the industry by garnering gold and platinum albums, million-selling singles, and U.S. then European tours; he kept blowing people's minds with hits by Love Unlimited, "Love's Theme" from the Love Unlimited Orchestra, and his own hits. This is the same Barry White from the ghetto, the child of destiny, who still bought clothes off the rack during the first few years of his success, who happily paid $1.9 million to the IRS in 1974 because he remembered all too well the welfare checks when there was no food on the table. By the early '80s, Barry's worldwide recognition stemmed from his unique brand of love music that broke down

cultural barriers in the Far East, Africa, America, the Caribbean, and Europe. But simultaneously, Barry faced personal changes: The death of his friend and partner Larry Nunes, shifts in musical styles and listening habits, and the tragic death of his only brother Darryl.

In 1986, after a two-year break, Barry came back with a new recording deal with A&M Records. His first album, "The Right Night & Barry White," caused the industry to sit up and take notice again. Young hit makers Big Daddy Kane, Lisa Stansfield, and Jazzie B. of Soul II Soul named him a major influence. In 1989, Quincy Jones called him to the studio to record "Secret Garden" alongside El DeBarge, Al B. Sure! and James Ingram. The tune became the bedroom song of 1989, the same year Barry released another album, the appropriately titled "The Man Is Back," which he followed with an international tour of Europe, Scandinavia, and the Mediterranean.

With the dawn of the '90s, Barry found himself recording with the likes of Big Daddy Kane and Isaac Hayes on tracks from his new album, "Put Me In Your Mix." Barry also received his due with the release of a three-disc boxed set, "Just For You," which brings back all the memories and '70s hits from the original King Of Bedroom Soul, whose influence can be heard on the contemporary hits of everyone from R. Kelly to Jodeci to Gerald Levert.

In 1994, Barry White is finally proclaiming that love is the icon. His new album on A&M, aptly titled "The Icon Is Love," is a concept album devoted to romance, sex, relationships, new beginnings and sad endings. Barry is at home and in the mix with producers Jimmy Jam & Terry Lewis, Gerald Levert & Tony Nicholas, Chuckii Booker, and partner Jack Perry.

"You have to have a commitment to consistency, you have to have dedication, and you have to have loyalty to those people who are important to you," says Barry of his long-term success. "You must have the desire to succeed along with the ability at whatever it is you want to succeed at."

BARRY WHITE DISCOGRAPHY

ALBUMS:

Released on 20th Century:

I've Got So Much To Give	1973
Stone Gon'	1973
Can't Get Enough	1974
Just Another Way To Say, I Love You	1975
Barry White's Greatest Hits, Vol. 1	1975
Let The Music Play	1976
Is This Whatcha Wont?	1976
Barry White Sings For Someone You Love	1977
The Man	1978
I Love To Sing The Songs I Sing	1979
Barry White's Greatest Hits, Vol. 2	1980

Released on Unlimited Gold Records and currently distributed by Priority Records except The Best Of Love:

The Message Is Love	1979
Sheet Music	1980
The Best Of Love	1980
Barry & Glodean	1981
Beware!	1981
Change	1982
Dedicated	1983

Released on A&M Records:

The Right Night & Barry White	1987
The Man Is Back!	1989
Put Me In Your Mix	1991
The Icon Is Love	1994

Released on Mercury (a division of Polygram Records):

Just For You (Barry White Boxed Set)	1992
Barry White: All-Time Greatest Hits	1994

PRACTICE WHAT YOU PREACH

(Spoken over intro:)
So, what do you want to do?
I'm here baby; I'm ready baby.
I'm waiting on you…
Believe me, I am patiently waiting on you.

Words and Music by BARRY WHITE,
GERALD LEVERT and EDWIN "TONY" NICHOLAS

THERE IT IS

(Spoken over intro-rhythm only:)
Don't say anything, don't say one word.
Just lay here.
Just be there and let me unwind a little.
Seems like the day would never end. This is so nice.
This is so nice.
(Music begins:)
It really feels so good. I love to play all up in your hair.
Let me touch you and rub you all over.
Baby just lay there.
I'm starting to feel something that's really intensifying my body.
Makes me want to do all kinds of things to you.

Words and Music by BARRY WHITE,
GERALD LEVERT and EDWIN "TONY" NICHOLAS

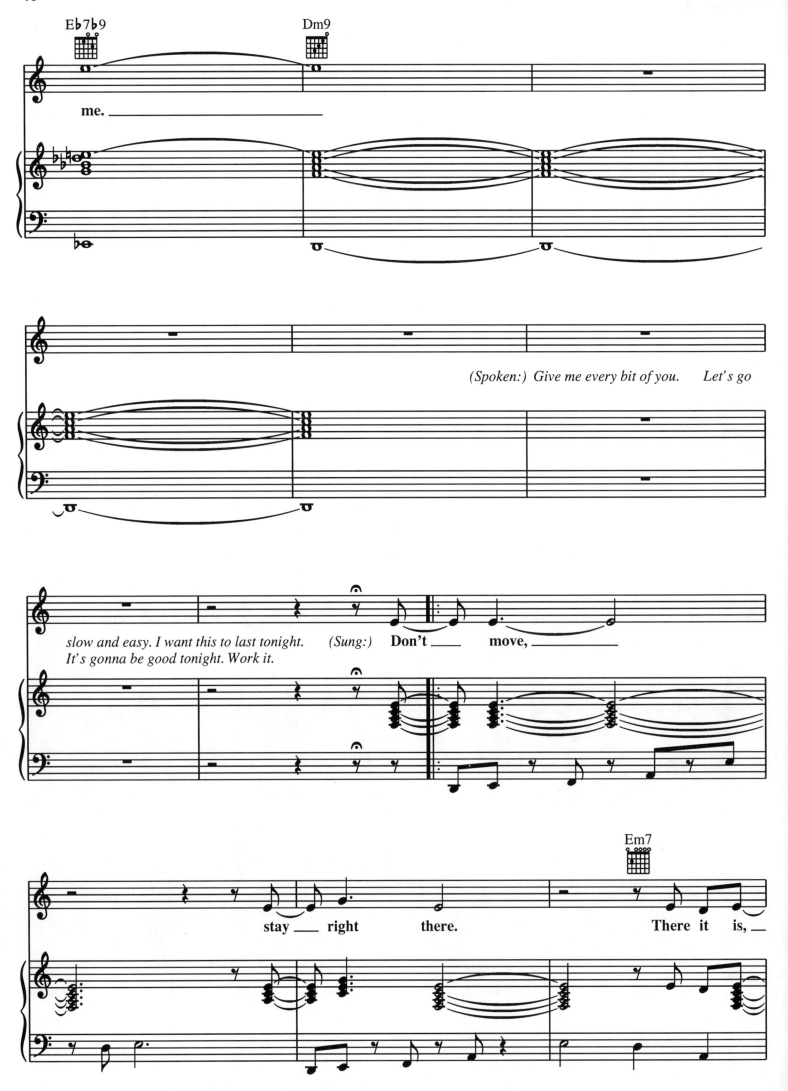

I ONLY WANT TO BE WITH YOU

(Spoken over intro:)
I know what I want.
Baby, I know what I like.
You're the one, you're my choice for life.
You, every bit of you;
I want it all, all of you.

Words and Music by BARRY WHITE,
JAMES HARRIS III and TERRY LEWIS

Slow funk

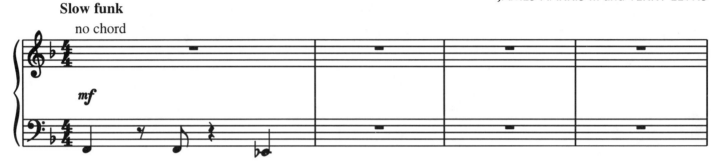

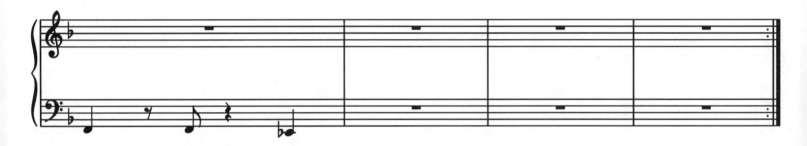

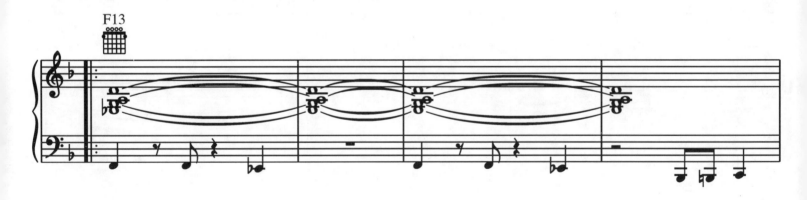

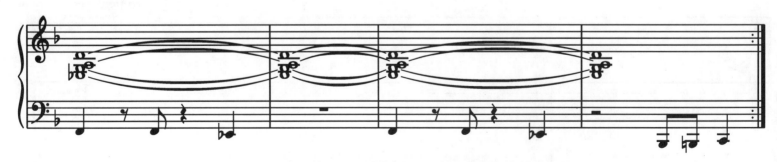

(Sung:) I want __ your love __ so bad __ it makes my
Girl, in __ my fan - ta - sies, __ I see

na - ture ache. __ Oh, let __ me share __ with you __
us to - geth - er. I'm lov - ing you, __ you're lov - ing me,

what - ev - er love it takes. I'll be __ your freak __
this could be for - ev - er. Make me __ your freak __

__ be - tween __ the sheets. __ It's what you do to me, __
__ be - tween __ the sheets. __ It's what you do to me, __

THE TIME IS RIGHT

Words and Music by BARRY WHITE
and CHUCKII BOOKER

BABY'S HOME

(Spoken over intro:)
Hey baby, it's so good to just stand here and look at you.
So many things are so different without you, because there's so many things so right about you.
Never again baby, ever again; and I love the way you feel in my arms,
Baby no one else has ever felt like this.

Words and Music by GARY BROWN,
BARRY EASTMOND and JOLYON SKINNER

(Sung:) I've ___ been a-way too long, my love. Your kiss tells me it's
Did ___ I hear you say, my love, your night's been long and

COME ON

(Spoken over intro:)
You're a freak, sweet freak.
You like to play hypnotic, erotic, sexy little games.
You like to play, just look at you;
All that movement, all those subtle little movements.
You like to play.
Baby believe me when I say I just
Love to play with you.

Words and Music by BARRY WHITE, JAMES HARRIS III,
TERRY LEWIS and JAMES WRIGHT

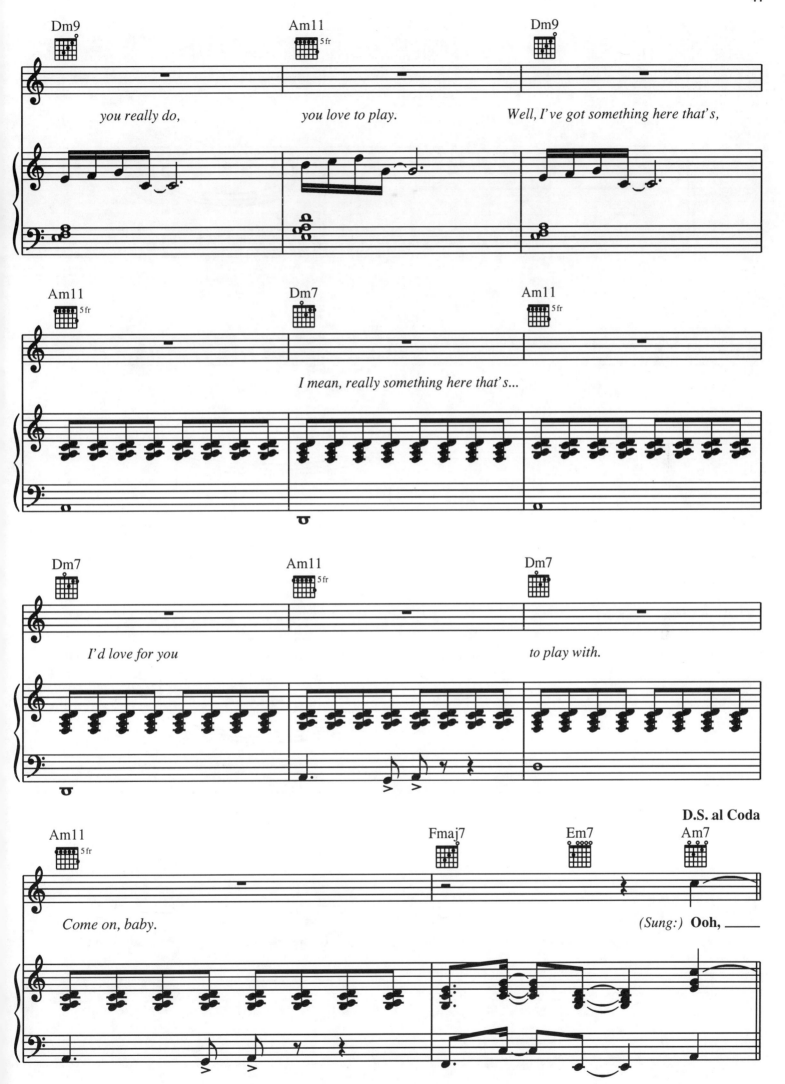

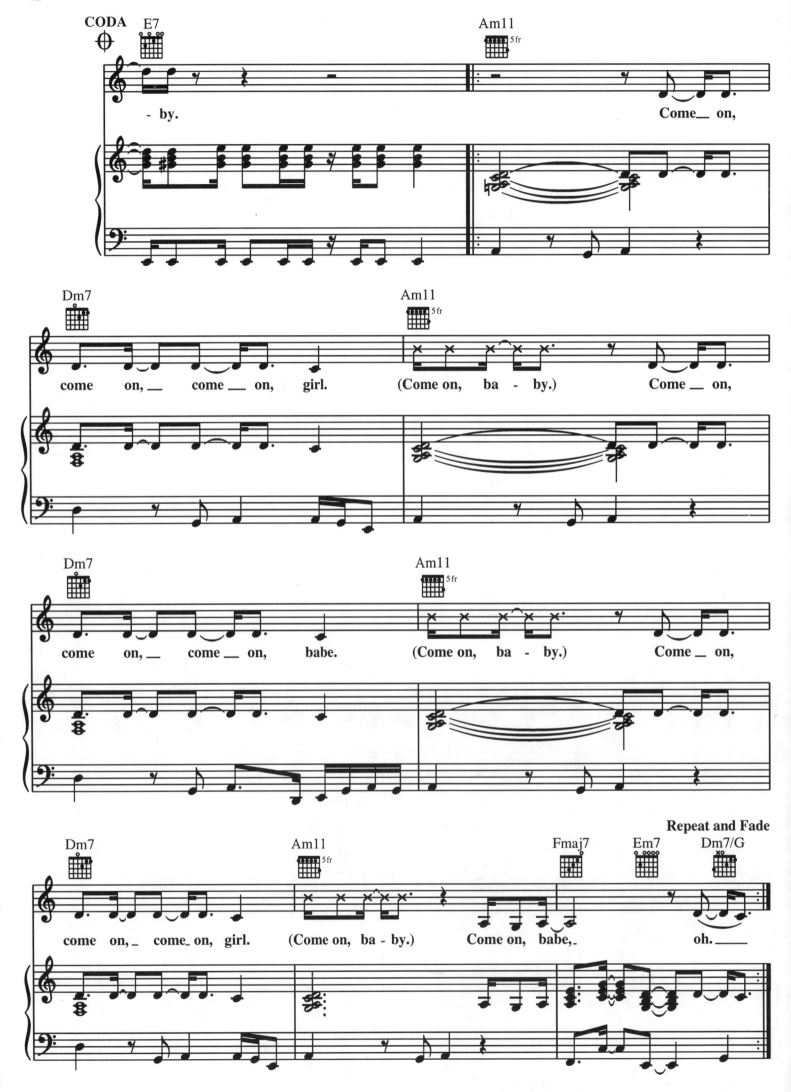

LOVE IS THE ICON

(Spoken over intro:)
Love is the icon and will always be the icon.
People all over the world
Searching, looking, trying to find love.
Love, love is not anything or something you can find yourself.
Most times it has to find you.
Yes that certain special feeling, yes, that we feel inside;
She makes you smile, she makes you feel a certain way.
He makes you feel good inside when he touches you.
Love truly is the icon.

Words and Music by BARRY WHITE
and JACK PERRY

SEXY UNDERCOVER

Words and Music by BARRY WHITE
and CHUCKII BOOKER

DON'T YOU WANT TO KNOW?

(Spoken over intro-no music:)
You know my feelings for you
Are getting stronger and stronger everyday,
And I'm learning more about you everyday.
And there's an area we need to address
Mentally, physically, and romantically immediately.
(Music begins:)
Tell me, show me all the little sensitive places
That make you feel the way you love to feel.
Baby I want to please you tonight.
Baby I really need you tonight.

Words and Music by BARRY WHITE
and MICHAEL LOVESMITH

Don't you want to know,_____ girl, if we_____ can fill_ the nights
know,_____ if we_____ can fill_ the nights

You won't answer me, but in your eyes I see   the answer is   very clear.

(Sung:) (Bring down the lights,   bring down the mu-sic.   Ba-by, let's bring down the house.)

WHATEVER WE HAD, WE HAD

(Spoken over intro:)
As the world turns from day to day, as we live we have to make decisions,
And when we make those decisions things don't always turn out the way we'd like them to or want them to.
No matter what we feel or what seems real, things change.
We don't have a crystal ball to look into to know what our future is going to be, or what it's gonna be.
You meet someone; you care for that someone, you love that one.
We made plans, we planned for so many things.
Life has always been that way so you must understand how I feel when I say we've had our run;
Good times, sad times, the fun times, the bad times.
We should always remember that we started as friends.
There's no reason we shouldn't end as friends, so whatever we had, we had.

Words and Music by BARRY WHITE
and MICHAEL LOVESMITH

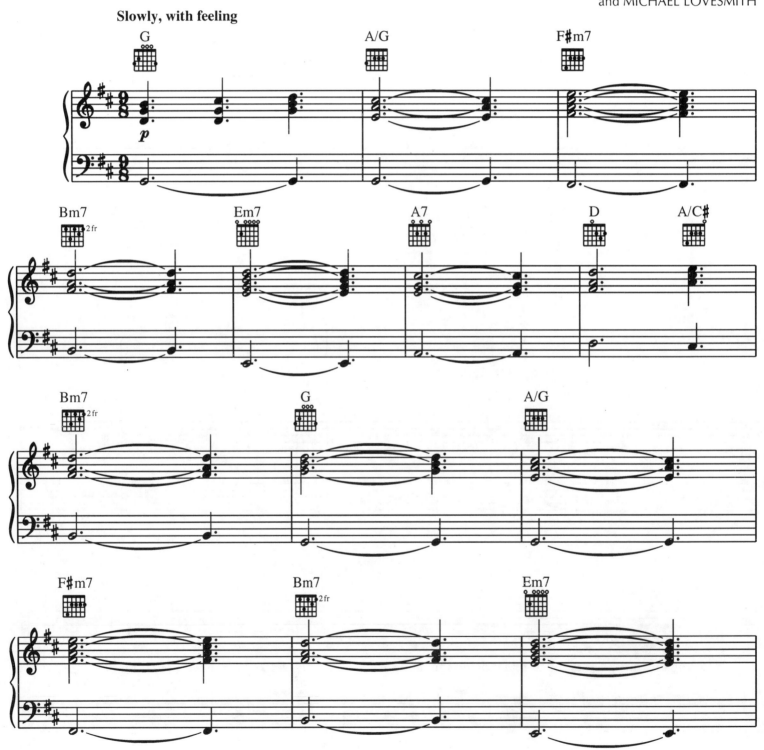

(Sung:) **What** ev – er _____ we
ev – er _____ we

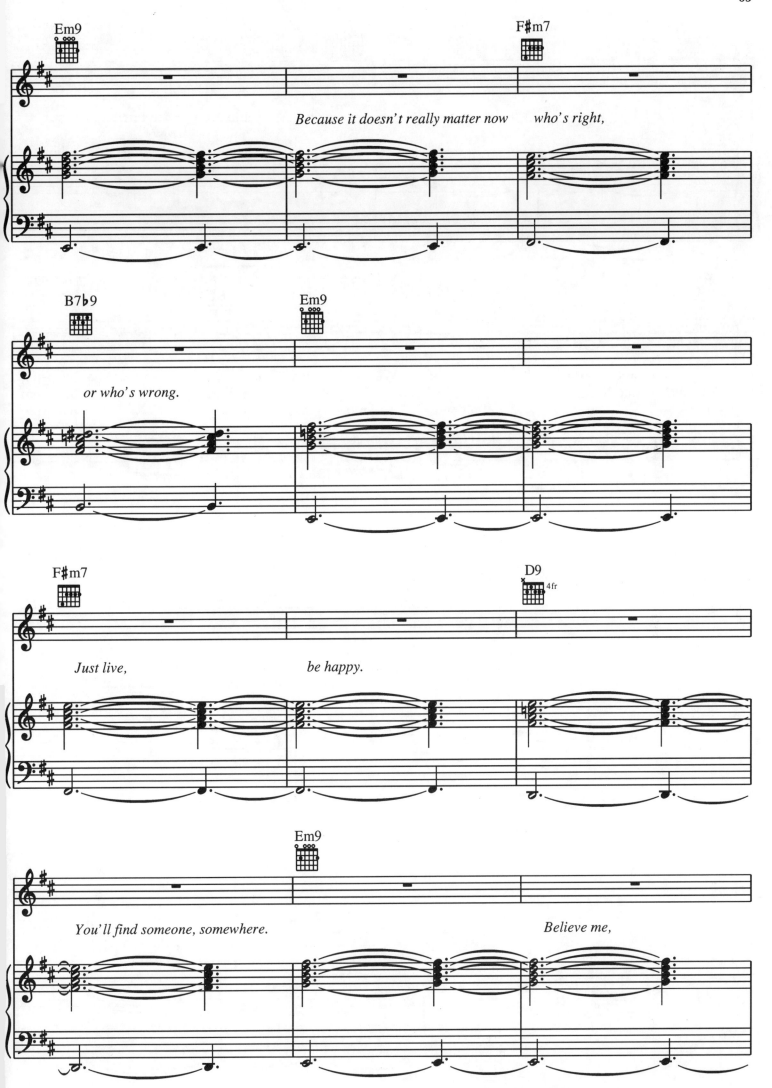